Profiles of the Presidents

LYNDON BAINES JOHNSON

★ ★ ★

Profiles of the Presidents

LYNDON BAINES JOHNSON

by Michael Burgan

Content Adviser: Harry Rubenstein, Curator of Political History Collections, National Museum of American History, Smithsonian Institution

Reading Adviser: Dr. Linda D. Labbo, Department of Reading Education, College of Education, The University of Georgia

COMPASS POINT BOOKS ✦ MINNEAPOLIS, MINNESOTA

Compass Point Books
3109 West 50th Street, #115
Minneapolis, MN 55410

Visit Compass Point Books on the Internet at *www.compasspointbooks.com*
or e-mail your request to *custserv@compasspointbooks.com*

Editors: E. Russell Primm, Emily J. Dolbear, Melissa McDaniel, and Catherine Neitge
Photo Researcher: Svetlana Zhurkina
Photo Selector: Linda S. Koutris
Designer/Page Production: The Design Lab/Les Tranby
Cartographer: XNR Productions, Inc.

Library of Congress Cataloging-in-Publication Data
Burgan, Michael.
    Lyndon Baines Johnson / by Michael Burgan.
      p. cm. — (Profiles of the presidents)
Summary: A biography of the thirty-sixth president of the United States, discussing his personal life, education, and political career.
Includes bibliographical references and index.
    ISBN 0-7565-0280-2 (alk. paper)
    1. Johnson, Lyndon B. (Lyndon Baines), 1908–1973—Juvenile literature. 2. Presidents—United States—Biography—Juvenile literature. [1. Johnson, Lyndon B. (Lyndon Baines), 1908-1973. 2. Presidents.] I. Title. II. Series.
    E847 .B87 2004
    793.923'092—dc21   2002153306

Table of Contents

★ ★ ★

*NOTE: In this book, words that are defined in the glossary are in **bold** the first time they appear in the text.*

Struggles of a Great Society

★ ★ ★

Lyndon Baines Johnson had dreamed about becoming president from the time he was a boy growing up in Texas. When he actually became president, however, Johnson faced many difficult problems.

Lyndon B. Johnson ▶ was sworn in as president aboard Air Force One after President Kennedy was shot and killed. Kennedy's widow, Jacqueline, stands to his left and his wife to his right.

At home, people were demanding **civil rights** for African-Americans. They wanted black Americans to be treated the same as white Americans. The United States was also locked in a struggle with the **Soviet Union** for political influence around the world. The Soviet Union practiced a form of communism in which the Communist party leaders controlled all levels of government and the economy. The United States wanted to stop communism from spreading.

▲ *At the time Johnson became president, many African-Americans like this young marcher in Washington, D.C., were fighing for equal rights.*

Johnson had mixed success in solving these problems. He sent half a million troops to fight in the Southeast Asian nation of South Vietnam to stop a communist government from taking power there. Over time, however, many Americans became angry that the United States was involved in this fight halfway around the world. Back in the United States, Johnson hoped to build a "Great Society" that would reduce poverty, improve education,

Johnson shaking ▶
hands with
supporters in
Providence, Rhode
Island, in 1964

and end **discrimination.** Johnson's plans helped decrease poverty and protect the rights of African-Americans.

Johnson was a man of strong emotions. He was committed to helping the poor and promoting civil rights. He could be generous and friendly. Unfortunately, he also had an explosive temper, and he did not handle criticism well. He believed he knew the answer to every problem, and he was sure his ideas would make him one of the greatest presidents ever to hold office.

Instead, Johnson is remembered as someone who helped promote civil rights for all minorities, but who also led the United States into an unpopular war.

Life in Texas

★ ★ ★

Lyndon Johnson's family had its roots in Texas. His grandfather, Sam Ealy Johnson Sr., owned a cattle ranch there. His mother's father, Joseph Baines, was a lawyer and a teacher. Lyndon's mother, Rebekah, was a journalist—an unusual job for a woman at the start of the twentieth century.

◄ Joseph Baines was a lawyer and a teacher.

In 1904, Lyndon's father, Sam Ealy Johnson Jr., won a seat in the Texas state **legislature**. Shortly after, he was interviewed by Rebekah Baines. The two fell in love.

Rebekah Baines ▲
Johnson was
a journalist.
Sam Ealy Johnson
Jr. worked as a
real estate agent,
farmer, and Texas
state legislator.

They married in 1907. On August 27, 1908, their first child, Lyndon, was born. In time, the Johnsons would have four more children, one boy and three girls.

Lyndon spent his first years on a farm near Stonewall, in central Texas. When he was five, his family moved to nearby Johnson City, though they later returned to Stonewall. During Lyndon's childhood, his father was elected to the state legislature six times. In between, he farmed and sold real estate. The family, however, was not wealthy. Lyndon did not grow up with electricity or indoor plumbing.

As a boy, Lyndon showed a quick mind. By the time he was three, he had memorized long poems. He loved to talk and could be very persuasive. A childhood friend later recalled, "Lyndon could talk my parents into anything, letting us do anything and go anywhere." That skill helped Lyndon in his political career.

◀ *Lyndon B. Johnson at eighteen months old*

Lyndon was a popular and gifted student. In 1924, he graduated from high school. Three years later, he enrolled in Southwest Texas State Teachers College. He

◀ *Johnson (far right) with two of his sisters and his baby brother in 1914*

Johnson with ▲
his sixth and
seventh grade
students in
Cotulla, Texas

had to work to pay for his classes. One of his most interesting jobs was teaching at a school in Cotulla, Texas. Most of the students were poor Mexican-Americans. Johnson said later, "I was determined to spark something inside them, to fill their souls with ambition and interest and belief in the future."

During his college years, Johnson also edited the school newspaper and led a group of students who were active in school politics. After graduating in 1930, he soon found himself starting his own career in politics.

To Washington

★ ★ ★

During the summer of 1930, Johnson spoke at a **campaign** rally. Without using any notes, he delivered a rousing speech that stirred the crowd. He caught the attention of Welly K. Hopkins, a local politician. Hopkins asked Johnson to manage his campaign. Johnson agreed, and Hopkins won the race.

◄ Welly K. Hopkins (left) and Johnson pose for a picture at the Empire State Building in New York.

Johnson was working as a high school teacher in Houston when he got his next political job. Richard Kleberg, a wealthy Texas rancher, had just been elected to the U.S. House of Representatives. Kleberg asked Johnson to serve as his secretary in Washington, D.C.

Always full of energy, Johnson devoted long hours to his new job. He learned who was important in Washington and how to deal with them. Johnson became friendly with Sam Rayburn, another Texan who later served as

Johnson became good friends with Sam Rayburn (right), shown in this 1954 photo.

Speaker of the House of Representatives, the top position in the House. Throughout his career, Johnson worked closely with more experienced leaders, studying their actions and gaining their trust.

In 1934, Johnson met Claudia Taylor, who came from a wealthy Texas family. Within two months, Johnson and Lady Bird, as Claudia was known, were married. Lady Bird joined Johnson in Washington. The couple returned to Texas the next year, where Johnson took a job with a new government agency. It was called the National Youth Administration (NYA), and it helped young people find work or continue their education.

By that time, the United States was in the middle of the Great Depression, a severe economic crisis. During the

▼ *The Johnsons on their honeymoon in Mexico in 1934*

During the depression, many people lost their jobs and lived in poverty. Photographer Dorothea Lange took this picture of a migrant family from Amarillo, Texas, outside their trailer home.

depression, millions of Americans lost their jobs and homes. To help these people, President Franklin D. Roosevelt started a group of programs that included the NYA. These programs were known as the **New Deal.** The New Deal was meant to improve the economy and

for dy ndon with another handshake
for franklin [signature]

◄ *President Franklin D. Roosevelt (left), Texas governor James V. Alfred, and U.S. Representative Lyndon B. Johnson in Galveston, Texas, in 1937; the president signed the photo for Johnson.*

to help the poor, but often its programs only helped poor white people. Johnson went out of his way to make sure African-Americans and Mexican-Americans in Texas received their fair share of the NYA's help.

By 1937, Johnson was ready for a new job. When a seat became vacant in Texas, he ran for the U.S. House of Representatives, saying he would support Roosevelt and the New Deal. Johnson won, and he soon met President Roosevelt. The young representative quickly developed a strong relationship with the president.

During World War II, Johnson served as a lieutenant commander in the Pacific.

In Congress, Johnson made sure farmers in Texas received government aid. He also supported a plan that brought electricity to certain parts of Texas for the first time. When voters back home wrote to him with a problem, Johnson always responded right away and took quick action. His goal, he later said, was to "always be the people's congressman, representing all the people, not just the ones with money and power." In 1941, Johnson ran for the U.S. Senate in a special election. The race was close, but he lost.

That December, the United States entered World War II (1939–1945). Johnson was the first member of Congress to sign up to join the military. Lady Bird ran his Washington office while he served with the U.S. Navy in the Pacific. His job was to report on the fighting taking place in the region. It wasn't long before Johnson and other congressmen were ordered back to Washington.

The war years were busy for Johnson and his wife. In 1943, they used some money that Lady Bird had inherited to buy a radio station in Austin, Texas. Later, they bought a television station, as well. These stations were successful and provided a good source of money for years to come. In 1944, the Johnsons had their first child, Lynda Bird. Their other daughter, Luci Baines, was born three years later.

▼ *The Johnson family, including daughters Lynda Bird (left) and Luci Baines in 1948*

Harry Truman became ▶
president when
Franklin D. Roosevelt
died in 1945.

The war ended in 1945, the same year President Roosevelt died, and his vice president, Harry Truman, became president. In 1948, Johnson again ran for the Senate. At the time, the Republican Party was weak in Texas. The Democratic **candidate** usually won the election. To win support, Johnson traveled across the state by helicopter, a rare form of transportation in the 1940s. People came out to hear him speak—and to see this new

flying machine. In September, Johnson won a close vote to become the Democratic candidate for senator. He easily won the November election.

In the Senate, Johnson managed to win the support of party leaders, and he quickly became an important figure in the Senate. By 1952, he was the leader of the Democrats in the Senate. Then, in 1954, the Democrats won more seats in the Senate than the Republicans. Johnson became the majority leader, the most powerful position in the Senate.

As Senate majority leader, Johnson played an important role in deciding which bills, or proposed laws, would be

◄ *Johnson during his campaign for the U.S. Senate in 1948*

▲ *Senate majority leader Lyndon B. Johnson greeting Senator Homer Ferguson (right) and Speaker of the House Sam Rayburn (center) at the White House in 1954*

voted on. Johnson became famous for making deals with senators. He would do favors for them if they supported bills he wanted made into laws. Johnson also used his speaking skills, intelligence, and charm to persuade others to do what he wanted. His methods were sometimes called the

Johnson and Senator ▾
Leverett Saltonstall,
a Massachusetts
Republican, reading
President
Eisenhower's 1957
budget plan

THE BUDGET
OF THE
UNITED STATES GOVERNMENT
FOR THE FISCAL YEAR ENDING JUNE 30
1957

Budget Message of the President
and
Summary Budget Statements

◄ *President Dwight
D. Eisenhower
worked closely
with Johnson.*

Johnson Treatment. Senator Hubert Humphrey of Minnesota
described Johnson's approach: "He'd come on just like a tidal
wave sweeping all over the place. . . . There was nothing deli-
cate about him." Johnson was one of the most powerful and
skillful Senate majority leaders ever to have served.

At that time, Dwight D. Eisenhower, a Republican,
was president. Johnson tried to work with Eisenhower.
He supported the way the president was dealing with the
Soviet Union. He also promoted the exploration of space.

Under Johnson's leadership, the Senate passed the first civil rights law since Reconstruction, the period just after the Civil War. Johnson's support of the Civil Rights Act of 1957 angered many southern Democrats. Many Southerners opposed any new civil rights laws. At the same time, many Northerners thought the 1957 law did not do enough to help African-Americans.

Johnson's fast pace and lifestyle—he was a heavy smoker—almost cut short his stay in the Senate. In July 1955, he suffered a major heart attack. He spent a month in the hospital and did not return to the Senate until January. Johnson quit smoking, lost weight, and tried to slow down, but he remained driven to succeed in his job. He also thought about running for president.

In the summer of 1956, the Democrats met to select their presidential candidate. Johnson was in the running, but the vote went to former Illinois governor Adlai Stevenson. For the next four years, Johnson continued to lead the Senate. Late in 1959, Sam Rayburn and others formed a group to support Johnson in the 1960 presidential election. Johnson wanted to be president, but he wasn't sure the time was right. At the same time, Democratic senator John F. Kennedy of Massachusetts was

traveling across the country, giving speeches and winning support. That summer, Kennedy became the
Democratic candidate for president. He asked Johnson
to run with him as the candidate for vice president.

◀ *Johnson and Lady
Bird shortly after his
heart attack in 1955*

Second in Command

★ ★ ★

In many ways, John F. Kennedy was a good choice for the Democrats in 1960. He had popular ideas, was young and handsome, and he had served his country during World War II. However, Kennedy was a Roman Catholic, and no Catholic had ever been elected president. Many Protestant Americans—particularly in the South—feared a Roman Catholic might put his religious beliefs before the best interests of the country. By choosing Johnson as his running mate, Kennedy hoped to win the support of Southerners and others who were not sure they wanted to vote for a Catholic. During the campaign, Johnson gave many speeches in the South. He helped convince some Democrats there to remain loyal to the party. In November, Kennedy won in a close race. Johnson would soon be the vice president of the United States.

John Adams, the nation's first vice president, had once called that position "the most insignificant office" in the U.S. government. Johnson hoped to make the vice presidency a more important job. Kennedy helped by giving Johnson responsibilities that most vice presidents had

◄ *John F. Kennedy (right) and Lyndon B. Johnson campaigning in front of Texas's state capitol in 1960*

not been given. Johnson often met with Kennedy and his cabinet, or close advisers. He attended meetings of the National Security Council, which advises presidents on military affairs. Johnson headed groups that studied space and civil rights issues. He also traveled around the world representing the U.S. government. Johnson later said, "President Kennedy was very good to me and tried his best to elevate the office any way he could."

President Kennedy (left) expanded the vice president's responsibilities.

Compared to the power Johnson once had in the Senate, however, he sometimes felt left out in his new position. He also knew that some of Kennedy's closest advisers—including his brother, Robert Kennedy—did not like him. Still, the vice president remained loyal to Kennedy, even though, as he later said, "I detested every minute of it."

▲ *Robert F. Kennedy did not always agree with Johnson.*

On November 21, 1963, Johnson greeted President Kennedy as he arrived in Texas. The president had come to raise money for the Democratic Party. Johnson was eager to entertain Kennedy at his ranch. He had planned a party for the night of November 22. The celebration never took place.

On that afternoon, as Kennedy was riding in a car through the streets of Dallas, he was shot and killed. Johnson was a few cars behind the president. A **Secret Service** agent covered Johnson's body with his own, trying to protect him in case more shots were fired. There were no more. Within an hour, Kennedy was dead. Johnson was soon sworn in as president.

Johnson spoke to the nation, honoring Kennedy and trying to ease Americans' pain. He said he hoped Kennedy's death would make Americans "one people in our hour of sorrow."

Kennedy riding ▶
through the streets of
Dallas a few minutes
before he was
shot and killed on
November 22, 1963

Kennedy had been popular, and Johnson worried that many Americans would not accept him as their leader. He was afraid people would study his every move and attack him

▲ *President Lyndon B. Johnson during a televised speech shortly after Kennedy's death*

quickly if he did something wrong. "The whole thing was almost unbearable," he later said.

Johnson decided to keep Kennedy's cabinet. He wanted to assure America and the world that the U.S. government would still work smoothly. In his first few weeks in office, Johnson spoke to leaders from business, labor groups, and the civil rights movement. He asked for their support during that difficult time.

Johnson also launched an investigation into Kennedy's murder. Many people thought there had been a plot to kill Kennedy. Some Americans thought Johnson himself might have been part of it. Others said the Soviet Union was involved. Johnson wanted to end these rumors, but the results of the investigation still raise questions to this day.

Early Success

★ ★ ★

Johnson followed through on some of Kennedy's plans. He worked for a tax cut and led what he called a war on poverty. The number of people living in poverty had fallen steadily after World War II, but under Kennedy it had begun to rise again. The war on poverty was part of Johnson's plan to build a Great Society. In 1964, Johnson said, "The Great Society rests on **abundance** and liberty for all. It demands an end to poverty and racial injustice, to which we are totally committed in our time." In some ways, the Great Society was Johnson's way to expand Roosevelt's New Deal.

In 1964 and 1965, the government started a number of programs that tried to help people find jobs and end poverty. Some programs offered job training. Food stamps, which helped poor families buy food, were introduced. Schools received billions of dollars. Volunteers in Service to America (VISTA) signed up young people to help provide assistance in poor communities. Not all these programs worked as well as Johnson had hoped. Still, the best of them did give useful aid to the poor.

◄ *A VISTA volunteer helped build a house in North Carolina in 1964 as part of Johnson's war on poverty.*

In discussing the Great Society, Johnson was trying to convince Congress to pass a new civil rights law. He worked with both Democrats and Republicans and refused to give in on key parts of the bill. The resulting Civil Rights Act of 1964 did more to protect the rights of African-Americans than any other law in American history. It outlawed discrimination in hotels, motels, restaurants, theaters, and other public places. In 1964 in the South, many black and white students were forced to attend separate schools. The new law helped end this and also banned discrimination in the workplace.

Johnson signing ▾ the Civil Rights Act of 1964

In some ways, Johnson had an easier time in Washington because of Kennedy's murder. Congress was more willing to work with the new president because the country had just gone through such a difficult time. However, Johnson knew that this good relationship would not go on forever. He needed a strong victory in the 1964 presidential election to continue his plans for the Great Society. The

▲ *Barry Goldwater lost to Johnson in the 1964 presidential election.*

Republican candidate that November was Senator Barry Goldwater of Arizona. Goldwater had voted against the Civil Rights Act of 1964. He talked openly about using **nuclear weapons** against the Soviet Union. During his campaign, Johnson suggested Goldwater would be a poor leader. He said Goldwater might do things that would hurt the country. Johnson easily defeated Goldwater, winning 61 percent of the votes. On January 20, 1965, Johnson was sworn in for a full four-year term as president.

Trouble at Home and Abroad

★   ★   ★

Johnson's full term began with more successes at home. His new Great Society programs included Medicare and Medicaid, which helped the elderly and the poor pay their medical bills. Johnson also called for a new civil rights act to end practices in the South that kept blacks from voting.

Secretary of Health, Education, and Welfare John Gardner discussing Medicare ▶

Overseas, however, President Johnson faced increasing troubles. In the 1950s, Vietnam had split into two countries. North Vietnam had become communist. South Vietnam was not communist, but its leaders were **corrupt.** A small group of powerful men there controlled the government.

▲ *Ho Chi Minh was North Vietnam's leader.*

By the time President Kennedy had taken office, South Vietnam was at war. Some South Vietnamese, known as the Vietcong, were fighting their government. They wanted to end their leaders' corrupt rule and start a communist government. North Vietnam supported this effort. They received help from the Soviet Union. Kennedy wanted to help South Vietnam fight the Vietcong. He sent money and military advisers to South Vietnam.

South Vietnamese ▶
president Ngo
Ding Diem

When Johnson became president, he continued to aid
South Vietnam. Johnson believed that if one country
became communist, neighboring countries would as well.
He also did not want other nations to think Americans
would not stand up against communists. If they did, he
said, "We would . . . find it impossible to accomplish anything for anybody anywhere on the entire globe."

During Johnson's first year as president, the United States increased its military activity in Vietnam. In August 1964, U.S. naval ships took part in a spy mission in the Gulf of Tonkin, off North Vietnam. The ships came under fire. Two nights later, the ships believed they were under North Vietnamese attack once again. Johnson used

▼ *Navy jets are ready for takeoff from the* USS *Constellation during the Gulf of Tonkin incident.*

that second attack—which never actually happened—as an excuse to bomb North Vietnam. He also asked Congress to approve further military actions. Congress gave Johnson the power he wanted to expand the war.

At first, Johnson ordered raids and more bombing. Then, in 1965, Johnson decided to send U.S. troops to help the South Vietnamese fight the war. By the end of the year, almost two hundred thousand American troops were in South Vietnam. Over time, Johnson sent more troops. Still, the North Vietnamese and Vietcong kept fighting back.

The war created problems for President Johnson at home. At first, most Americans supported the war. Slowly, however, more people said the war should end. Johnson did not want to back down in Vietnam, but he did not want deeper U.S. involvement.

Starting in 1965, many young people began to protest against the war. They did not want young Americans fighting in South Vietnam. Some protesters were against the idea of the U.S. government supporting the corrupt South Vietnamese government. Others were against war in general. At some protests, tens of thousands of people marched in the streets.

Some taunted the president, shouting, "Hey, hey, LBJ, how many kids did you kill today?" Johnson couldn't stand being criticized. "Don't they know they're American?" he asked his aides. He thought the protesters were being disloyal to their country. However, many Americans who loved their country

▾ *U.S. soldiers come ashore in South Vietnam in 1965.*

Veterans marched ▲ to the Pentagon in Washington, D.C., in protest of the Vietnam War.

questioned why U.S. troops were being killed to defend South Vietnam.

At home, civil rights remained a difficult issue. Many African-Americans were demanding the same rights and opportunities as everyone else. They looked to civil rights leaders, such as the Reverend Martin Luther King Jr., to challenge discrimination. King often led protest marches. In Selma, Alabama, marchers were

★

protesting rules that kept them from voting. In 1965, Selma police officers attacked marchers. Many blacks were clubbed, and a white minister was killed. These protests strengthened Johnson's belief that Congress had to pass the Voting Rights Act of 1965. This act ended many state and local laws that kept African-Americans from voting. In spite of Johnson's efforts to improve civil rights, the violence did not end.

▲ *Martin Luther King Jr. speaks to a rally of marchers in Selma, Alabama, in 1965.*

During the summer of 1965, riots erupted in Watts, a black neighborhood in Los Angeles. The next two summers, frustrated African-Americans rioted in several cities. Some people were protesting the poverty in their lives or the harsh treatment they received from white police officers. The worst riots came in 1967. Detroit, Michigan, was especially hard hit, and Johnson sent in

U.S. troops to restore order. Later, the president formed a group to find out why the riots had occurred, although he already had an idea. He later said, "As I see it, I've moved the [African-American] from D+ to C-. He's still nowhere. He knows it. And that's why he's out in the streets. . . . I'd be there, too."

A report on the riots advised spending more money to fund Great Society programs. However, the country was already spending billions of dollars on the war in Vietnam. Johnson could not spend as much as he wanted to fight poverty. Still, he tried to improve relations between whites and blacks. In 1967, he named Thurgood Marshall the first black justice on the U.S. Supreme Court.

▼ *Thurgood Marshall was the first African-American justice on the U.S. Supreme Court.*

The Final Years

★ ★ ★

By the end of 1967, polls showed that almost half of Americans wanted the country to pull out of the Vietnam War. In the 1968 presidential election, Johnson faced a challenge from another Democrat. Senator Eugene McCarthy of Minnesota wanted to become president so he could end the

Senator McCarthy campaigned to end the war in Vietnam.

Vietnam War. Presidents seeking reelection usually don't have to run against someone from their own party. McCarthy's campaign showed how deeply split the country was over the war.

The bad news for Johnson continued in 1968. On January 31, Vietcong and North Vietnamese forces launched surprise attacks on dozens of South Vietnamese cities. The communists lost most of the battles, but the attacks stunned Americans. A few weeks later, Johnson learned that another Democrat, Robert Kennedy, was going to challenge him for the presidency.

By March 31, Johnson had made two important decisions. He would stop most of the bombing in North Vietnam in order to pursue peace talks. He also told the nation he would not run for reelection. Friends said that after his announcement he looked relieved. The Vietnam War had weakened his presidency—and his will to stay in politics.

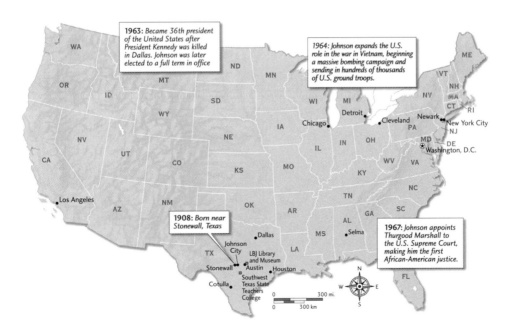

1963: Became 36th president of the United States after President Kennedy was killed in Dallas. Johnson was later elected to a full term in office

1964: Johnson expands the U.S. role in the war in Vietnam, beginning a massive bombing campaign and sending in hundreds of thousands of U.S. ground troops.

1908: Born near Stonewall, Texas

1967: Johnson appoints Thurgood Marshall to the U.S. Supreme Court, making him the first African-American justice.

The rest of the year was filled with violence at home and abroad. U.S. troops—now numbering more than five hundred thousand—kept on fighting in Vietnam. In April, Martin Luther King Jr. was assassinated. Two months later, Robert Kennedy was shot and killed as he campaigned for president. In August, Chicago police attacked protesters outside the building where the Democrats were choosing Hubert Humphrey (who had been Johnson's vice president) as their presidential candidate. In November, Johnson tried to end some of the violence, halting all bombing in North Vietnam. This came right before the presidential election,

Richard M. Nixon (left), Lyndon B. Johnson, Lady Bird Johnson, and Pat Nixon met at the White House shortly after Nixon's presidential victory in 1968. The Vietnam War did not end until Nixon's second term in office.

which Republican Richard Nixon won. Nixon promised he would end the Vietnam War, but fighting would drag on for several more years.

On January 17, 1969, Johnson spoke to the press for the last time as president. He told reporters, "I don't think my administration has done enough in hardly any field." Three days later, he and Lady Bird left the White House and returned to Texas. Johnson was looking forward to relaxing. "I just want to be lazy for a while," he told one reporter. For the next few years, he worked on his ranch and wrote about his presidency. He also raised money for a library that would hold his public papers.

By that time, Johnson was suffering from more health problems. On January 22, 1973, he suffered another heart attack and died at his ranch.

▲ *Lyndon B. Johnson and Lady Bird Johnson at their ranch in Texas in 1972*

Lyndon B. Johnson was a larger than life force in American politics. Although the Vietnam War tore his beloved country apart and tarnished his presidency, it is not his only legacy. Johnson took brave steps to help the poor, improve education, and promote racial equality. He is remembered for trying his best during extremely difficult times.

President Nixon ▼ placed a wreath at the foot of Lyndon B. Johnson's casket, which lay in state in Washington, D.C.

GLOSSARY

★ ★ ★

abundance—having plenty of something

campaign—an organized effort to win an election

candidate—someone running for office in an election

civil rights—legal protections for citizens

corrupt—willing to break laws to get money or power

discrimination—treating people unfairly because of their race, religion, sex, or age

legislature—the part of government that makes or changes laws

New Deal—President Franklin Roosevelt's group of programs to help people in need during the Great Depression

nuclear weapons—powerful bombs that use the power created by splitting atoms

Secret Service—the government agency in charge of protecting the president

Soviet Union—a communist nation formed in 1922 when Russia combined with fourteen other republics in eastern Europe and central Asia; it broke apart in 1991

LYNDON BAINES JOHNSON'S LIFE AT A GLANCE

★ ★ ★

PERSONAL

Nickname: LBJ

Born: August 27, 1908

Birthplace: Near Johnson City, Texas

Father's name: Samuel Ealy Johnson Jr.

Mother's name: Rebekah Baines Johnson

Education: Graduated from Southwest Texas State Teachers College in 1930

Wife's name: Claudia Alta "Lady Bird" Taylor Johnson (1912–)

Married: November 17, 1934

Children: Lynda Bird Johnson (1944–), Luci Baines Johnson (1947–)

Died: January 22, 1973, near Johnson City, Texas

Buried: Near Johnson City, Texas

PUBLIC

Occupation before presidency: Teacher, public official

Occupation after presidency: Retired

Military service: U.S. Navy during World War II

Other government positions: Representative from Texas in the U.S. House of Representatives; U.S. senator from Texas; vice president

Political party: Democrat

Vice president: Hubert H. Humphrey (1965–1969)

Dates in office: November 22, 1963– January 20, 1969

Presidential opponents: Barry M. Goldwater (Republican), 1964

Number of votes (Electoral College): 43,129,566 of 70,307,754 (486 of 538), 1964

Writings: *The Vantage Point: Perspectives on the Presidency (1963–69)* (1971)

Secretary of state:
  Dean Rusk (1963–1969)

Secretary of the treasury:
  C. Douglas Dillon (1963–1965)
  Henry H. Fowler (1965–1968)

Secretary of defense:
  Robert S. McNamara (1963–1968)
  Clark M. Clifford (1968–1969)

Attorney general:
  Robert F. Kennedy (1963–1965)
  Nicholas Katzenbach (1965–1967)
  Ramsey Clark (1967–1969)

Postmaster general:
  John A. Gronouski (1963–1965)
  Lawrence F. O'Brien (1965–1968)
  W. Marvin Watson (1968–1969)

Secretary of the interior:
  Stewart L. Udall (1963–1969)

Secretary of agriculture:
  Orville L. Freeman (1963–1969)

Secretary of commerce:
  Luther H. Hodges (1963–1965)
  John T. Connor (1965–1967)
  Alexander B. Trowbridge (1967–1968)
  Cyrus R. Smith (1968–1969)

Secretary of labor:
  W. Willard Wirtz (1963–1969)

Secretary of health, education, and welfare:
  Anthony J. Celebrezze (1963–1965)
  John W. Gardner (1965–1968)
  Wilbur J. Cohen (1968–1969)

Secretary of housing and urban development:
  Robert C. Weaver (1966–1969)
  Robert C. Wood (1969)

Secretary of transportation:
  Alan S. Boyd (1967–1969)

LYNDON BAINES JOHNSON'S LIFE AND TIMES

★ ★ ★

JOHNSON'S LIFE	WORLD EVENTS

August 27, Johnson is born near Johnson City, Texas — **1908**

1910

1909   The National Association for the Advancement of Colored People (NAACP) is founded

1913   Henry Ford begins to use standard assembly lines to produce automobiles (below)

1916   German-born physicist Albert Einstein (below) publishes his general theory of relativity

JOHNSON'S LIFE

WORLD EVENTS

1919   World War I
(1914–1918) peace
conference begins at
Versailles, France

1920   1920   American women get
the right to vote

1929   The United States
stock exchange
collapses and severe
economic depression
sets in

Graduates from   1930   **1930**   1930   Designs for the first
Southwest Texas State   jet engine are
Teachers College   submitted to the
Patent Office in
Britain

Becomes secretary to   1931
Representative Richard
M. Kleberg (below)

1933   Nazi leader Adolf
Hitler (below) is
named chancellor
of Germany

JOHNSON'S LIFE		WORLD EVENTS

November 17, **1934**
marries Claudia Alta
"Lady Bird" Taylor

Appointed by Franklin **1935**
D. Roosevelt (below,
left) as Texas state
administrator of the
National Youth
Administration

1935 George Gershwin's
opera *Porgy and Bess*
opens in New York

Wins a seat in the **1937**
U.S. House of
Representatives

1939 German troops
invade Poland (above);
Britain and France
declare war on
Germany; World
War II begins

The film *The Wizard
of Oz* is released

JOHNSON'S LIFE

1940

WORLD EVENTS

1941   December 7, Japanese bombers attack Pearl Harbor, Hawaii (left), and America enters World War II

1944   DNA (deoxyribonucleic acid) is found to be the basis of heredity

1945   America drops atomic bombs on the Japanese cities of Hiroshima and Nagasaki to end World War II

Elected to the   **1948**
U.S. Senate

1949   Birth of the People's Republic of China

1950

Becomes the leader   **1953**
of the Democrats in
the Senate

1953   The first Europeans climb Mount Everest (right)

Becomes Senate   **1955**
majority leader

1955   Disneyland, the first theme park in the United States, opens in Anaheim, California

1958   The Guggenheim Museum in New York opens

1959   Fidel Castro becomes prime minister of Cuba

Barbie doll debuts

JOHNSON'S LIFE

1960

Becomes vice president   1961

November 22, is   1963
sworn in as president
(above) after John F.
Kennedy is killed

Announces his war on
poverty

Presidential Election Results:		Popular Votes	Electoral Votes
1964	Lyndon B. Johnson	43,129,566	486
	Barry M. Goldwater	27,178,188	52

July 2, signs the Civil   1964
Rights Act ending
legal discrimination
in public places

August 7, Congress
gives Johnson the
power to send U.S.
troops into the
Vietnam War

WORLD EVENTS

1961   Soviet cosmonaut Yuri
Gagarin is the first
human to enter space

The Berlin Wall is
built, dividing East
and West Germany

1962   Rachel Carson's
influential book *Silent
Spring* is published,
increasing environ-
mental awareness
nationwide

1963   Kenya becomes an
independent republic
(its first president,
Jomo Kenyatta, is
pictured below)

1964   G.I. Joe makes his
debut as the first boy's
"action figure"

JOHNSON'S LIFE

Signs the Voting Rights
Act, which outlaws
certain rules that kept
African-Americans
from voting — 1965

Appoints Thurgood — 1967
Marshall the first
African-American U.S.
Supreme Court justice

Signs the Civil — 1968
Rights Act of 1968,
ending discrimination
in real estate

March 31, announces
he will not run for
another term

May 13, peace talks
between the United
States and North
Vietnam begin

November 1, orders a
halt to all bombing in
North Vietnam

January 22, suffers a — 1973
heart attack and dies

WORLD EVENTS

1966 — The National
Organization for
Women (NOW) is
established to work for
equality between
women and men

1968 — Civil rights leader
Martin Luther King Jr.
(below) is assassinated

1969 — U.S. astronauts are the
first humans to land
on the Moon (below)

1973 — Arab oil embargo
creates concerns about
natural resources

1970

UNDERSTANDING LYNDON BAINES JOHNSON AND HIS PRESIDENCY

★ ★ ★

IN THE LIBRARY

Colbert, Nancy A. *Great Society: The Story of Lyndon Baines Johnson.*
Greensboro, N.C.: Morgan Reynolds Publishing, 2002.

Joseph, Paul. *Lyndon B. Johnson.* Minneapolis: Abdo & Daughters, 2000.

Maupin, Melissa. *Lyndon Baines Johnson: Our Thirty-Sixth President.*
Chanhassen, Minn.: The Child's World, 2002.

Shuman, Michael A. *Lyndon B. Johnson.* Springfield, N.J.:
Enslow Publishers, 1998.

ON THE WEB

The American President—Lyndon B. Johnson
http://www.americanpresident.org/KoTrain/Courses/LBJ
For in-depth information about Johnson and his presidency

Internet Public Library—Lyndon Baines Johnson
http://www.ipl.org/div/potus/lbjohnson.html
For quick facts and links to other resources

The American Experience—Vietnam
http://www.pbs.org/wgbh/amex/vietnam/
To learn more about the Vietnam War and its
effects on the United States during Johnson's presidency

JOHNSON HISTORIC SITES
ACROSS THE COUNTRY

Lyndon B. Johnson National Historical Park
P.O. Box 329
Johnson City, TX 78636
830/868-7128
http://www.nps.gov/lyjo/
To visit Johnson's boyhood home and the ranch where he later lived

Lyndon Baines Johnson Library and Museum
2313 Red River St.
Austin, TX 78705
512/721-0200
To find out more about Johnson and his times

THE U.S. PRESIDENTS
(Years in Office)

★ ★ ★

1. George Washington
   (March 4, 1789-March 3, 1797)
2. John Adams
   (March 4, 1797-March 3, 1801)
3. Thomas Jefferson
   (March 4, 1801-March 3, 1809)
4. James Madison
   (March 4, 1809-March 3, 1817)
5. James Monroe
   (March 4, 1817-March 3, 1825)
6. John Quincy Adams
   (March 4, 1825-March 3, 1829)
7. Andrew Jackson
   (March 4, 1829-March 3, 1837)
8. Martin Van Buren
   (March 4, 1837-March 3, 1841)
9. William Henry Harrison
   (March 6, 1841-April 4, 1841)
10. John Tyler
    (April 6, 1841-March 3, 1845)
11. James K. Polk
    (March 4, 1845-March 3, 1849)
12. Zachary Taylor
    (March 5, 1849-July 9, 1850)
13. Millard Fillmore
    (July 10, 1850-March 3, 1853)
14. Franklin Pierce
    (March 4, 1853-March 3, 1857)
15. James Buchanan
    (March 4, 1857-March 3, 1861)
16. Abraham Lincoln
    (March 4, 1861-April 15, 1865)
17. Andrew Johnson
    (April 15, 1865-March 3, 1869)

18. Ulysses S. Grant
    (March 4, 1869-March 3, 1877)
19. Rutherford B. Hayes
    (March 4, 1877-March 3, 1881)
20. James Garfield
    (March 4, 1881-Sept 19, 1881)
21. Chester Arthur
    (Sept 20, 1881-March 3, 1885)
22. Grover Cleveland
    (March 4, 1885-March 3, 1889)
23. Benjamin Harrison
    (March 4, 1889-March 3, 1893)
24. Grover Cleveland
    (March 4, 1893-March 3, 1897)
25. William McKinley
    (March 4, 1897-
    September 14, 1901)
26. Theodore Roosevelt
    (September 14, 1901-
    March 3, 1909)
27. William Howard Taft
    (March 4, 1909-March 3, 1913)
28. Woodrow Wilson
    (March 4, 1913-March 3, 1921)
29. Warren G. Harding
    (March 4, 1921-August 2, 1923)
30. Calvin Coolidge
    (August 3, 1923-March 3, 1929)
31. Herbert Hoover
    (March 4, 1929-March 3, 1933)
32. Franklin D. Roosevelt
    (March 4, 1933-April 12, 1945)

33. Harry S. Truman
    (April 12, 1945-
    January 20, 1953)
34. Dwight D. Eisenhower
    (January 20, 1953-
    January 20, 1961)
35. John F. Kennedy
    (January 20, 1961-
    November 22, 1963)
36. Lyndon B. Johnson
    (November 22, 1963-
    January 20, 1969)
37. Richard M. Nixon
    (January 20, 1969-
    August 9, 1974)
38. Gerald R. Ford
    (August 9, 1974-
    January 20, 1977)
39. James Earl Carter
    (January 20, 1977-
    January 20, 1981)
40. Ronald Reagan
    (January 20, 1981-
    January 20, 1989)
41. George H. W. Bush
    (January 20, 1989-
    January 20, 1993)
42. William Jefferson Clinton
    (January 20, 1993-
    January 20, 2001)
43. George W. Bush
    (January 20, 2001-)

INDEX

★ ★ ★

ABOUT THE AUTHOR

Michael Burgan is a freelance writer of books for children and adults. A history graduate of the University of Connecticut, he has written more than sixty fiction and nonfiction children's books for various publishers. For adult audiences, he has written news articles, essays, and plays. Michael Burgan is a recipient of an Edpress Award and belongs to the Society of Children's Book Writers and Illustrators.